Books, Stories
and Puppets

Ready, Steady, Play!

Series Editor: Sandy Green

Guaranteed fun for children and practitioners alike, the Ready, Steady, Play! series provides lively and stimulating activities for children.

Each book focuses on one specific aspect of play offering clear and detailed guidance on how to plan and enjoy wonderful play experiences with minimum fuss and maximum success.

Each book in the Ready, Steady, Play! series includes advice on:

- How to prepare the children and the play space
- What equipment and materials are needed
- How much time is needed to prepare and carry out the activity
- How many staff are required
- How to communicate with parents and colleagues

Ready, Steady, Play! helps you to:

- Develop activities easily, using suggested guidelines
- Ensure that health and safety issues are taken into account
- Plan play that links to the early years curriculum
- Broaden your understanding of early years issues

Early years practitioners and students on early years courses and parents looking for simple, excellent ideas for creative play will love these books!

Other titles in the series

Construction 1-84312-098-4 Boyd
Creativity 1-84312-076-3 Green
Displays and Interest Tables 1-84312-267-7 Olpin
Festivals 1-84312-101-8 Hewitson
Food and Cooking 1-84312-100-X Green
Music and Singing 1-84312-276-6 Durno
Nature, Living and Growing 1-84312-114-X Harper
Role Play 1-84312-147-6 Green
Play Using Natural Materials 1-84312-099-2 Howe

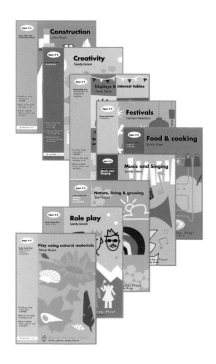

Books, Stories and Puppets

Sandy Green

David Fulton Publishers

To Jasmine and Harry, who love stories and a visit from Granny's puppets.

And to Alfie. who will soon be joining in the fun.

David Fulton Publishers Ltd
The Chiswick Centre, 414 Chiswick High Road, London W4 5TF

www.fultonpublishers.co.uk

First published in Great Britain in 2006 by David Fulton Publishers

10 9 8 7 6 5 4 3 2 1

Note: The right of Sandy Green to be identified as the author of this work has been asserted by her in accordance with the Copyright, Designs and Patents Act 1988.

David Fulton Publishers is a division of Granada Learning Ltd, part of ITV plc.

British Library Cataloguing in Publication Data
A catalogue record for this book is available from the British Library.

ISBN 1-84312-148-4

Typeset by FiSH Books, London
Printed and bound in Great Britain

Contents

Books, Stories and Puppets

Welcome to *Books, Stories and Puppets*, an exciting new publication which is part of the Ready, Steady, Play! series.

Get ready to enjoy a range of activities with your children, which will stimulate their all-round development.

The Ready, Steady, Play! books will help boost the confidence of new practitioners by providing informative and fun ideas to support planning and preparation. The series will also consolidate and extend learning for the more experienced practitioner. Attention is drawn to health and safety, and the role of the adult is addressed.

How to use this book

Books, Stories and Puppets is divided into five main sections.

Section 1 provides background information on the value of books and story-telling to young children, both planned and unplanned opportunities. Ideas are given for making story-time both visual and creative, and also on holding children's attention.

Section 2 presents a selection of visual images to help initiate discussion with children about well-known stories and story-book characters. Each photograph or illustration will be familiar to most children and each will  feature later in the book within the activity section. These visual prompts help support children in observation and memory, in taking ideas forward, in initiating ideas for story-time and as preparation for a story-based activity.

Section 3 includes a selection of well-known and much-loved tales and stories. Each book is briefly outlined and presented with a selection of linked activities. These activities provide practitioners with ideas to build upon each story-book, using it as the central theme for topic work, or simply as a pleasurable creative activity.

Section 4 provides suggestions for visual resources linked to and in support of stories (e.g. making puppets, storyboards, changeable wall displays, story sacks and using Persona dolls). The simple-to-follow guidelines will hopefully entice even the most reluctantly creative practitioner to think, 'Yes, I can do that'.

The photocopiable templates in Section 5 support the creation of many of the various activities and props suggested throughout the book. They are cross-referenced for ease of use. Many may be easily adapted for readers' own requirements.

Finally a list of useful books, resources and stockists is given on pp. 95–6. This list is by no means definitive but should act as a good starting point.

So read on, and enjoy ... **Ready, Steady, Play!**

Sandy Green
Series editor

Acknowledgements

Thanks to the following for letting me include examples of their products:

- Milet Publishing Ltd, specialists in dual language books.
- Mantralingua, specialists in dual language books.
- Storysack®.

The images of 'Living Puppets' are included by kind permission of Puppets By Post. 'Living Puppets' are copyright Matthies Spielprodukte GmbH & Co KG, Hamburg.

Thanks also to Harry and Helen at Oldfield Park Bookshop for always finding me a copy of whatever I need, and to Noah's Ark Nursery, Midsomer Norton and Little Learners Nursery, Radstock, for providing photographs on p. 30 and p. 68 respectively. Thanks and admiration go to nursery nurse Annette Walkey of Little Bridges Nursery, Wadebridge Community Primary School who, with help from class teacher Delyth Griffith and parents, made the wonderful story sacks on p. 65.

Series acknowledgement

As series editor I would like to thank the children, parents and staff at:

- The Nursery and Reception class, Wadebridge Community Primary School, Wadebridge, Cornwall
- Happy Days Day Nursery, Wadebridge, Cornwall
- Snapdragons Nursery, Weston, Bath, Somerset
- Snapdragons Nursery, Grosvenor, Bath, Somerset
- Tadpoles Nursery, Combe Down, Bath, Somerset

for letting us photograph their excellent provision, resources and displays.

Thanks also to John and Jake Green, Jasmine and Eva for their help throughout the series, and to Nina, Margaret and Ben at David Fulton Publishers for their patience, enthusiasm and support.

Introduction

Stories form part of the heritage of every culture, being passed down from generation to generation. Throughout history books have been considered as precious items, often hidden during times of conflict and limitation. The impact of books upon our lives is immeasurable. The impact of books and stories upon a child's development is equally immeasurable. For children to learn to read they usually need to develop within an appropriate environment. They need to have adults who are willing to sit and talk with them, helping them to build on their vocabulary. They need to see the written word around them in all its forms, in books, newspapers and magazines, on notices, signposts, headings and instructions, in letters, on postcards, and on menus and receipts. They need to develop an understanding about when the written word is used, how it is used and its potential impact upon their lives. They need to experience the pleasures and uses of books, and other written forms, and to see adults clearly demonstrating this around them by using literature in everyday life.

As adults we turn to literature for many reasons: for factual information, for exploration of ideas, as an individual experience and as a shared time with others. Literature gives us pleasure and enhances our lives in so many ways.

For children it can also help them make sense of their world and the new experiences they come across. For example, reading or hearing stories about the arrival of a new sibling, a house move or hospital stay, the death of a relative or family pet, or even a visit to the dentist, hairdresser or doctor can help them understand that others have similar feelings and concerns, and wonder about the same things. These opportunities can help dispel anxiety and turn potentially negative experiences into more positive ones.

Exploration of books and literature helps develop concentration skills and the understanding that print has meaning, and that both print and illustrations are symbols, representing aspects of a story or information. It is generally accepted that children who are surrounded by and have easy access to books and other written material, and who enjoy listening to stories regularly, are often the more successful readers in later years. It is easy to see how restricted access to literature in all its forms is likely to place limitations on a child's capacity to learn and experience in a supportive and reassuring manner.

Every adult can provide literary experiences of some kind or other for young children. It is not essential that adults can read themselves. Those with competent literacy skills can of course read to children one-to-one or in groups, enjoying the illustrations with them and perhaps demonstrating how the text is followed. Those with less well-developed literacy skills can verbally retell tales they know well, using their personal enthusiasm and eye contact to keep the children focused and interested.

Planning and preparation of the environment

Think about where the children see the written word around your setting. Hopefully you will have clear labels on:

- coat pegs
- name cards
- storage boxes
- welcome signs
- posters
- displays, paintings and other creative work

Other opportunities to demonstrate to children that print carries meaning include:

- newsletters to parents
- a general information board
- a food allergy board

Setting up a book area

Preparing the book and story-telling corner is extremely important. A comfortable area with carpeting, cushions and/or comfy chairs will invite children to snuggle up with a book, either alone or with a friend. It will also feel calming to them as they are seated for a group activity. Positioning the book area slightly apart from the main hustle and

bustle of the rest of the room helps produce a peaceful environment where children are less likely to be distracted.

What books?

The choice of books available today is enormous, and selecting a range for young children can be an absolute delight, but there are also pitfalls. Books that are not suitable for the developmental stage of the children in your care are less likely to be so enjoyable or meaningful to them. It is important that you consider the age/s and stage/s of the children you are providing for. This ensures that they enjoy experiences at a level appropriate for them.

Remember:

- The younger the child, the shorter the story should be. This is a good 'rule of thumb' to guide you.
- Young children love repetition – they find both pleasure and security in the familiarity of well-loved stories.
- Consider the clarity of the pictures – Will they appeal to the children? Are they meaningful and relevant?

- Often, clear, bold text is best for young children.

- The general appearance and front cover of a book is vital – Does it shout 'Pick me up' when you look at it?

- Durability is important – Books made of durable materials with good-quality paper and bindings are best for little hands learning how to handle books carefully.

- Consider the story content carefully – Is it clear? Is it relevant?

- Consider (whenever appropriate) if the story is emotionally satisfying (i.e. any action or drama would usually have a climax and a positive ending).

- Are the portrayed images positive? Does the book give positive messages? It is important to ensure that the books you provide include adults and children of both sexes and all cultures being equally valued, and that stereotyping of gender or race is avoided. Be particularly careful if you are given books from well-meaning parents or other adults. Stereotyping was rife just a few years ago in children's books.

- Include books in dual languages. This is vital to support children whose first language is not English. It will enable parents speaking that language to read to their child and others in their heritage tongue, and will also teach the children that text can be read in different ways, not only from left to right as in English.

Shown in
English/Chinese

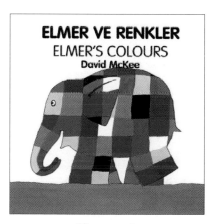

Shown in
English/Turkish

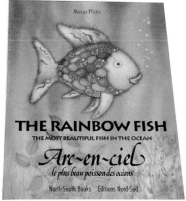

Shown in
English/French

- Include books that deal with emotions such as jealousy, anger, sadness and fear. This helps the children to explore and come to terms with situations and experiences.

- Include books that support topic work (e.g. books on diggers and tractors would be useful within a topic on transport or farming). Similarly, a book on birds would support a topic on flight or nature, or one on clothing could link well with festivals or people.
- Include books that:
  - Are factual
  - Are fictional
  - Pass on heritage
  - Show similarities between cultures
  - Are in more than one language
  - Are beautiful to look at and handle
  - Are both fun and funny
  - Provide a sense of adventure
  - Introduce children to poetry and rhymes.

Dual language books

It is important to include books in a range of languages whenever possible, particularly those representative of the languages spoken within the setting. Whenever possible also include picture dictionaries and alphabet books, books which depict other cultures, traditional tales from other cultures, and books that show similarities between cultures.

Displaying books

Books can be set out on shelves, on tables, in racks, mobile boxes or on hinged shelving. Whatever type of storage you use, ensure that the books are presented carefully and tidily. This will encourage a respect for the written word in your children.

Ensure that shelving is secure and does not tip as smaller children reach up to the highest rack or shelf. Hinged shelving should be positioned so that accidental closure of the structure is impossible.

If you are lucky enough to have 'Big' books, again they need to be stored carefully to encourage proper use and easy access.

Story-telling

Within your planning remember to include:

- One-to-one story time – giving individual children some special time with an adult's undivided attention. It is amazing (and very sad) how many children do not experience this at home.
- Easy access to books throughout the day – ideally children will be able to sit down with a book whenever they wish.

- Group story-time – a wonderful opportunity to experience a shared pleasurable activity.
- Books as a reference source – with the growing impact of ICT, don't forget to help children experience the benefits of using books for reference. This is particularly useful during topic work and when putting together a display.

- The use of props – Puppets, sound-making items or relevant artefacts can enhance a story. They can also keep an easily distracted child more focused, or the fiddlers' hands occupied.

- The involvement of drama – Making story-time active can be great fun. This works particularly well with the most familiar tales, such as *The Three Little Pigs*, and well-loved books such as *Going on a Bear Hunt* (see example on p. 30).

- Persona dolls – These wonderful resources, first developed by Babette Brown, can help with the smooth integration of a new child, or the prevention or resolution of a sensitive situation within an early years setting (see pp. 69–70 for more information).

- Storyboards – a wonderful way to involve children in the representing of a story they have enjoyed, or a familiar situation (see pp. 62–3, which provides ideas to get you started).

- Wall displays where 'things' change! This is a wonderful way of monitoring children's observation skills. The anticipation of what might happen next can cause great excitement (see p. 68 for ideas and photographs of a successful example which caused much excitement).

The role of the adult

As well as providing a safe environment for children, the adult has other important roles too. These include:

- Reading stories with enthusiasm, never boredom or distraction.

- Maintaining control of large groups through careful planning of stories appropriate to the group's needs and attention span.

- Ensuring all the children are settled before you start.

- Always reading a new story in advance to be certain you know how the story goes, its suitability for the children in your care and any surprises that may crop up. I know of an NQT who read *The Elephant and the Bad Baby* by Elfrida Vipont and Raymond Briggs, adding in the word 'Please' all the way through because she thought it sounded better. Readers familiar with the story will already understand the impact of this 'error' upon the story as a whole. Readers unfamiliar with it – check it out when you get a chance.

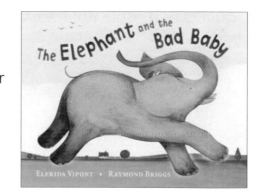

- Discussing stories with the children. What did they like best? What do they think will happen next? What can they tell you about the progression of the story? What happened at the beginning, what about the middle, and what was the conclusion? Who were the heroes, and (where applicable) who were the villains? Which bits made them laugh? What (if anything) might cause sadness? Why?

- Using strategies to distract 'wanderers' to avoid disrupting the flow of the story for the rest of the group.

- Being seen to use books as a reference themselves.

- Encouraging the use of books for reference purposes throughout the setting (e.g. when a caterpillar is brought in for observation, or a child returns from a holiday somewhere exciting, during topic work as support material for displays, and simply when a child asks a question that can trigger the use of a reference book).

- Giving praise and encouragement to children as they access information from written sources.

- Giving praise and encouragement to children as they attempt to write within their play, and in labelling their work and creative items.

- Encouraging language use and vocabulary extension whenever appropriate through discussion and open questioning.

- Planning activities carefully, providing the necessary equipment for linked activities.

- Providing sufficient resources for each activity, including material for supporting the development of writing skills relevant to the activity (e.g. labels, tickets, food orders).

If possible, try changing the role-play area into a library or a bookshop and take time to explore with the children how books are stored in categories and alphabetically.

Ensure that a range of pre-reading activities are provided across the setting to enable children to develop the skills they will need, for example:

- Games such as picture lotto or dominoes help them compare and match.

- Jigsaw puzzles require shape identification and fine motor manipulation.

- Sorting activities develop observation skills and the ability to repeat a sequence.

- Games such as 'Pairs' or picture snap also involve using memory and matching skills.

Each of these examples provides opportunities for children to develop and build on their pre-reading skills.

Health and safety

Attention to health and safety is important to all aspects of early years provision. Relevant points have been indicated as appropriate for the activities in this book. As a general rule, the book and story-telling area should be kept clean, tidy and hazard-free. There should be sufficient space for children to sit comfortably. All shelving and other storage must be secure.

When encouraging creativity in children linked to the activities in this book, all paints, glues and so on must be non-toxic, scissor use must be carefully supervised and use of items such as staplers should be limited to adults.

Links with parents/carers

If possible, encourage parents to take their children to the library to encourage reading as a habit. Suggest also that they explore books and other types of literature around their homes, perhaps sharing a favourite childhood story with their children, or telling them a well-known tale from their culture or another culture with which they are familiar.

Remember:

Children are never too young to start enjoying books.

Discussion resources

The following section provides a range of photographs and pictures of familiar items or characters from well-known stories. Many of these will be known to the children already. Which stories can they identify by looking at the pictures? What can they tell you about them?

These pages may be used to help children guess the story they are about to hear or to extend their learning through linked topic work.

Who is this? Who knows what happens to him in the story?

Who did these belong to? What happened?

Who might the building materials belong to? Why did they need them?

What is this? What can you tell me about this story?

What story involves a caterpillar? What does the caterpillar do?

What is this? What story includes these creatures? What can you tell me about the story?

What is this? What can you tell me about animals like this?
Can you think of a story which includes one of these animals?
What can you tell me about it?

What fruit can you see? Who can think of a story which involves fruit? Who has a favourite fruit?

Activities

The following pages contain twenty-three different activities linked to eight well-known and much-loved books, together with some additional ideas to extend topics further. Each activity follows a standard format to ensure ease of planning and implementation:

- the resources needed
- the aim(s)/concept(s)
- the process
- group size
- health and safety
- discussion ideas/language
- extension ideas
- links to the Foundation Stage Curriculum.

Key to Foundation Stage Curriculum abbreviations:

SS Stepping stones

ELG Early learning goals

PSE Personal, social and emotional development

CLL Communication, language and literacy

MD Mathematical development

KUW Knowledge and understanding of the world

PD Physical development

CD Creative development

STORY 1

The Giant Jam Sandwich

A delightful story in which the community pulls together to try to get rid of a swarm of wasps – the noisy, nasty nuisance. Written in amusing rhyme with busy and funny illustrations. A book which is great fun.

ACTIVITY 1

Weaving a checked tablecloth

Resources you will need

- Large rolls of two different coloured papers (green and white look good together)
- A small saw or old bread knife
- Adhesive tape and stapler

The Giant Jam Sandwich
Story and pictures by John Vernon Lord
with verses by Janet Burroway

Group size

1–2

Aim/concept

- To develop hand–eye co-ordination by weaving.

Links to Foundation Stage Curriculum

PD   Engage in activities requiring hand–eye co-ordination (SS)

ELG   Handle tools, objects, construction and malleable materials safely and with increasing control

Process

- Using the saw or knife cut the coloured paper into strips about 6cm wide.
- Cut out a large square of white paper and fold it in half and show the children how to cut slits across the folded paper, starting from the fold, leaving a 6cm border at the open edge.
- Open out the paper and support the children in weaving, helping them fix the ends securely.
- Use as part of a wall display linked to the story, or for a table display for dolls or other small world play.

Vocabulary/discussion

- Use terms such as under, over, through, overlapping, weaving, in and out

Extension idea

Make individual mats for use at home or at snack table

Health and safety

⚠ Adult only to use saw and stapler

ACTIVITY

2 Making sandwiches

Resources you will need

- Slices of bread
- Margarine
- Jam
- Plates
- Round-ended knives

Process

- Talk to the children about making a sandwich. Who has done it before? Encourage them to explain the process to you and to each other.
- If possible, make the bread with the children the day before.
- Ensure everyone washes their hands. Be seen to wash yours too.
- Provide the resources the children need. Support them in spreading margarine, spooning jam, cutting the sandwiches into shapes of their choice.
- Enjoy eating the sandwiches at snacktime.
- Talk about the difference between their sandwiches and the one in the story.

Aim/concept

- To make own snack, carrying out the process in the correct order

Vocabulary/discussion

- Introduce terms such as spreading, cutting, spooning
- Talk about colours and textures
- Talk about dietary needs and hygiene when cooking or preparing food
- If making bread talk about changes to the ingredients, the smell of the baking and so on

Group size

4–6

Extension ideas

1. Enjoy a picnic with families – make sandwiches as a group activity.
2. Make pretend sandwiches as a creative activity, using card, red and yellow tissue paper, material and so on.
3. Make a wall display of a giant plate of sandwiches.
4. Make wasps with the children using observation skills and memory. Provide yellow paper, black paint for the stripes, material for making wings, legs and so on.

Links to Foundation Stage Curriculum

PD Show awareness of a range of health practices with regard to eating, sleeping and hygiene (SS)

ELG Recognise the importance of keeping healthy and those things which contribute to good health

Health and safety

⚠ Careful supervision of knife use
⚠ Awareness of food allergies
⚠ Alternatives should be offered to children with gluten or lactose intolerances

The Gingerbread Man

A well-loved traditional tale in which children love to join in with its repetition 'Run, run, as fast as you can . . .'. Easy to link to a drama activity, cooking and food.

ACTIVITY

3

Making gingerbread men

Resources you will need

- Clean aprons and a cleaned cooking surface
- Access to a cooker, weighing scales, spoons and mixing bowl
- Plain flour, brown sugar, margarine, ground ginger, bicarbonate of soda, one egg and golden syrup
- Gingerbread man cutters and rolling-pin
- Currants or sweets for eyes and nose
- Copy of recipe card (optional) (p. 85)

Aim/concept

- To weigh, mix and make gingerbread men, exploring the effects of combining ingredients.

Process

- Talk about gingerbread men. Who has eaten them before? Who has made them? When? Where? What did they taste like?

- Ensure hands are washed well. Be seen to wash yours well, too.
- Talk through the ingredients and equipment. Which items can the children name?
- Show the children the recipe card (if using it). Talk about each stage in the process.
- Help the children weigh the ingredients. Encourage them to estimate which item will be heavier and so on.
- When the mixture is ready, give each child a small amount of dough to roll out, and provide them each with a cutter. Lay gingerbread people on baking try and place in oven.
- When cooked, leave to cool and then discuss the similarities and differences between each 'person' with the children before enjoying eating them.

Vocabulary/discussion

- Introduce terms such as weigh, mix, crack, blend, cream, stir, knead, roll.
- Discuss the changes in the ingredients as the dough begins to form, as well as taste, texture and smell, and comparison of features; eyes, nose, mouth, buttons.

Group size

4

Extension ideas

1. Make biscuit dough instead, using a range of different cutter shapes.
2. Use people cutters to make sandwiches.
3. Encourage children to draw each other, looking at similarities and differences, OR
4. Enlarge a gingerbread man cutter image for decorating.

Links to Foundation Stage Curriculum

MD   Order two items by weight or capacity (SS)

ELG   Use language such as 'greater', 'smaller', heavier' or 'lighter' to compare quantities

KUW   Show an awareness of change (SS)

ELG   Ask questions about why things happen and how things work

Health and safety

⚠ Ensure cooking surfaces are clean
⚠ Careful handwashing
⚠ Supervision throughout the process
⚠ Adult only to use cooker

ACTIVITY

4 Printing with cutters

Resources you will need

- Sheets of paper
- Gingerbread man cutters
- Dishes of medium thickness paint
- Aprons

Aim/concept

- To simply enjoy making 'people' patterns

Group size

4–6

Vocabulary/discussion

- Talk about individual features: eyes, nose, mouth, clothing items, body parts

Process

- Provide large sheets of paper and dishes of medium thickness paint.
- Encourage the children to make a people picture using gingerbread men cutters (no longer used for cooking activities).
- Encourage them to give them facial features, clothes and so on.
- Display the paintings on a wall.

Extension ideas

1. Look at paintings by L.S. Lowry with the children (e.g. http://www.lslowry.com). Encourage them to make matchstick people using their fingers to paint with.
2. Make a paper chain of people by drawing around cutters on to concertina folded paper and cutting them out, leaving a row of people 'holding hands', and use to decorate, count and so on.
3. Use puppets to help retell the story. Take turns being the main characters. If possible, provide puppets or finger puppets and a story tape to listen to as a free access activity.

Links to Foundation Stage Curriculum

CRE Use their imagination in art and design, imaginative and role play (ELG)

Goldilocks and the Three Bears

Everybody loves bears, and this timeless story provides scope for a range of activities. Explore emotions through empathy with Baby Bear (sadness, disappointment, confusion), and with Goldilocks (inquisitiveness, awe, fright). Make and mend items, and discuss the importance of privacy and why we shouldn't trespass.

ACTIVITY 5

Drama

Aim/concept

- To act out a story as a group, focusing on the story's sequence – beginning, main part, conclusion

Process

- Talk to the children about the story. How much can they tell you about it?
- As a group, lead the children through the main parts of the story, role playing each main action (e.g. making porridge, setting the table, going for a walk).
- Everyone be Goldilocks. Carry out each of her 'deeds'. Talk about how she may be feeling. What is she doing? Should she be doing it?
- Now be the three bears arriving home. Role play each bear in turn as they see their bowls, chairs and beds. Again, talk about how they may feel. How would the children feel if they were Baby Bear?
- Run away like Goldilocks, and let the bears (children) chase you!
- Talk to the children about what the bears should do next to repair the damage and replace the porridge.

Vocabulary/discussion

- Use emotional terms such as worried, cross, puzzled, angry, upset, frightened and so on
- Also talk about the story sequence – emphasise the start, the process and the end or conclusion

Group size

Whole group activity

Links to Foundation Stage Curriculum

CD Play co-operatively as part of a group to act out a narrative (SS)

ELG Use imagination in art and design (e.g. imaginative role play and stories)

Extension idea

Make masks to wear during role play.

Health and safety

⚠ Ensure that enough space is available for the free movement of the numbers of children involved

ACTIVITY 6

Making porridge

Resources you will need

- Clean aprons, cleaned cooking surfaces
- Saucepan and access to a cooker, OR a large bowl and access to a microwave
- A cup for measuring, oats, milk, water, sugar
- Jam or syrup (optional)
- Wooden spoons, small bowls for tasting
- Recipe card (optional) (see p. 86)

Aim/concept

- To combine ingredients for a purpose, measuring and weighing

Process

- Talk about porridge. Who knows what it tastes like? Who has it for breakfast? What do they like about it?
- Help the children measure or weigh the ingredients.
- Let the children take turns to mix the ingredients together.
- Cook the mixture in either the microwave or the saucepan.
- Leave standing until sufficiently cool to be eaten safely.
- Provide a choice of jam or syrup to add to the porridge.
- Enjoy tasting the porridge together.

Group size

4

Extension idea

Use porridge oats to make flapjacks or oatcakes

Vocabulary/discussion

- Talk about the measurements being used, the names of utensils and the ingredients
- Encourage the children to predict what will happen
- Introduce terms such as thicken, combine, gooey, lumpy, smooth

Health and safety

- ⚠ Ensure that all surfaces are clean
- ⚠ Careful supervision of handwashing
- ⚠ Adult only to have access to cooker or microwave
- ⚠ Ensure that porridge has cooled sufficiently before tasting takes place
- ⚠ Be aware of food allergies and offer an alternative if necessary

Links to Foundation Stage Curriculum

CLL Extend vocabulary, especially by grouping and naming (SS)

ELG Extend their vocabulary, exploring the meanings and sounds of new words

KUW Show an interest in why things happen and how things work (SS)

ELG Ask questions about why things happen and how things work

ACTIVITY 7
Making clay bowls for the bears

Resources you will need

- Clay boards, clay – air-dry clay will be useful if you wish the children to take the bowls home or keep them as permanent props.

Aim/concept

- To explore the properties of this natural material while shaping and designing an item for a purpose

Process

- Prepare the clay in advance, ensuring that it is suitable for the children to mould and handle. Press your finger against it; it should not be sticky or clinging.
- Give each child a small ball of clay and encourage them to explore it with their hands. How does it feel? Is it cool or warm? Does this change?
- Talk about the three bears' porridge bowls. What shape are they? How can that shape be achieved using the balls of clay in front of them?
- Discuss the picture on p.15. Which size bowl do they think they will make?
- Support the children in making their bowls then leave the bowls to dry.
- The bowls can be painted and/or varnished when firm.

Group size

4–6

Links to Foundation Stage Curriculum

PSE Persist for extended periods of time at an activity of their choosing (SS)

ELG Maintain attention, concentrate and sit quietly when appropriate

CD Use available resources to create props to support role play (SS)

ELG Use their imagination in art and design, imaginative and role play and stories

Vocabulary/discussion

- Introduce terms such as mould, squeeze, handle, press, pull, push, hard, soft, soften
- Talk about the changes experienced as the clay is handled. Does it soften, or does it dry out and become crumbly?

Extension idea

Provide a range of malleable materials and encourage the children to compare and contrast their uses (e.g. clay, dough, plasticine, fimo, kaylite)

Health and safety

⚠ Be aware of children with skin allergies; they may need to wear disposable gloves when handling clay

⚠ Clean all surfaces well afterwards to avoid leaving a dust layer

ACTIVITY 8
Collage pictures using textures

Resources you will need

- A range of textured material (e.g. fur, wool, felt, towelling, suede)
- A teddy bear and a bear shape for the children to observe (see p. 87)
- Scissors, pencils and glue

Aim/concept

- To make collage bears, exploring texture and colour, and using observation and manipulative skills

Vocabulary/discussion

- Use descriptive language (e.g. soft, furry, knobbly, silky, fuzzy, woolly)
- Name colours with the children, drawing their attention to differences in colour shades

Process

- Talk to the children about bears. What do they look like? How might they feel to touch? Who has a teddy bear at home? What is it made from? How does it feel to touch? What colour is it?
- Talk about the collage materials you have provided. Which are the children able to name? Encourage them to feel and describe each material in turn. Which do they like best? Why is that? What colours can they see?
- Provide a cut-out teddy bear shape for the children to use as a guide. Support them as necessary in drawing and cutting out their own bears.
- Encourage the children to make a collage of bears with material and leave to dry before mounting a display.

Group size

4–6

Extension ideas

1. Set up a textures table, encouraging the children to classify items by texture.
2. Label each texture (e.g. furry, bobbly).
3. Set up a table of children's and staffs' own teddy bears and put into order by size, or classify by colour, texture and so on.

Links to Foundation Stage Curriculum

KUW Describe simple features of objects and events (SS)
ELG Investigate objects and materials by using all of their senses as appropriate

Health and safety

⚠ Careful supervision of scissor use

The Three Little Pigs

Children love this traditional tale of good versus bad, with the pigs always being the winners. It provides opportunities to discuss right and wrong, helping other people and independence. Construction in its many forms can also be easily linked. The repetition of huffing and puffing and so on is always a firm favourite and can help entice even the most reluctant participants to join in the fun.

ACTIVITY

9 Drama

Resources you will need

- No essential resources needed, but bricks, sticks and straw could be incorporated as static props to guide the pigs from place to place around the room

Aim/concept

- To act out a story as a group, working together to overcome the wolf and focusing on the story's sequence – beginning, main part, conclusion.

Process

- Talk to the children about the story. How much can they tell you about it? Which part is their favourite?
- As a group, lead the children through the main parts of the story, role playing each main action (e.g. waving goodbye to mummy pig, meeting each man in turn, asking for and carrying off a pile of straw, sticks or bricks. Exaggerate the strength needed to carry each in turn).

- Role play each pig in turn, taking turns being a pig or a wolf. Model the appropriate actions for the children.
- All huff and puff like the wolf, trying to blow down the houses.
- Talk about how the pigs might be feeling. How would the children feel if the wolf was blowing their house down?
- Run away like the pigs as each house falls.
- Celebrate overcoming the wolf with dancing and singing.

Vocabulary/discussion

- Use terms such as design, carry, build, construct
- Name the materials: straw, sticks, bricks
- Refer to actions such as blowing, huffing, gasping, running
- Discuss emotions, sadness, excitement, feeling scared, relief and happiness

Group size

Whole group activity

Extension ideas

1. Provide a range of materials for the children to explore. See p.16 or provide a range of construction kits to build with.
2. Huff and puff into paper bags – who can fill them with air?
3. Move like a wolf on all fours and then like a pig on little trotters.

Links to Foundation Stage Curriculum

PD Negotiate space successfully when playing racing and chasing games with other children (SS)

ELG Move with confidence, imagination and in safety

CD Play co-operatively as part of a group to act out a narrative (SS)

ELG Use imagination in art and design, music, dance, imaginative role play and stories

Health and safety

⚠ Ensure that enough space is available for the numbers of children taking part in the activity

⚠ Careful supervision is needed if bricks, sticks and straw are positioned around the room

ACTIVITY 10 Constructing houses for the three pigs

Resources you will need

- A range of construction kits, plus other materials that may be used to find out what makes the strongest house (e.g. blocks, duplo, mega-blocks, constructo-straws, lolly sticks (from craft sources)). What other materials do you have?
- Small world pigs – preferably from a fairly large-scale farmyard set

Aim/concept

- To explore the properties of various construction materials, and to make a range of houses to find out which is the strongest

Process

- Set out the range of construction materials in advance.
- Talk to the children about them and explain that they are going to see which materials enable them to build the strongest house.
- Provide them with pigs to go in the houses.
- Give them freedom to experiment, but be on hand to guide and suggest as appropriate.
- Encourage the children to plan and predict.
- Give verbal prompts to help them reflect on their constructions.
- Display the range of houses, and discuss the strengths and weaknesses of each material type as a group.

Vocabulary/discussion

- Introduce terms such as build, construct, higher, wider, stable, unstable, strong, strengthen
- Make comparisons between sizes of structures and pigs
- Encourage planning terminology, e.g. If I . . . , we could . . . ; it might work if . . .

Group size

4 for each material if there is sufficient

Extension idea

1. Encourage the children to draw their structures, supporting them in representing their structures in both two and three dimensions.
2. If possible invite a builder to the setting to talk about their work.
3. Look at the building you are in and help the children note its features.

Links to Foundation Stage Curriculum

MD Show interest by sustained construction activity or by talking about shapes or arrangements (SS)

ELG Use everyday words to describe position

KUW Construct with a purpose in mind, using a variety of resources (SS)

ELG Build and construct using a wide range of objects, selecting appropriate resources, and adapting work where necessary

Health and safety

- ⚠ Ensure that children have plenty of space in which to experiment safely
- ⚠ Careful supervison of any high structures

Exploring materials

Resources you will need

- Small pieces of brick, stick, straw, tiles, a perspex tile (or a glass tile if safety glass is used)
- Water tray, weighing scales, torches and sheets of cardboard
- This activity will benefit from more than one adult being available

Aim/concept

- To explore what each material can do e.g. Which will float? Which will sink? Which is heaviest? Which is lightest? Which will let water through? Which will let light through?

Group size

Two children at each activity, preferably two adults moving between the activities

Process

- Prepare the four activity areas in advance.
- Draw the children's attention back to the houses built by the 3 pigs. What can they tell you about each material?
- Show them the range of materials. Which ones did the pigs use?
- Refer to each prepared activity area in turn: water tray, weighing scales, torches and boards, perspex (or glass) tile. What do they think they might try and find out in each activity area?
- Support the children as they experiment, encouraging descriptions and new vocabulary.

Vocabulary/ discussion

- Introduce terms such as floating, sinking, porous, water-resistant, heaviest, lightest, transparent
- Ask the children to try and anticipate the outcome, or predict which material will sink the quickest

Links to Foundation Stage Curriculum

CLL Use talk to connect ideas, explain what is happening and anticipate what might happen next (SS)

ELG Use talk to organise, sequence and clarify thinking, ideas, feelings and events

KUW Examine objects and living things to find out more about them (SS)

ELG Find out about, and identify, some features of living things, objects and events they observe

Extension ideas

Provide a range of both natural and man-made items to continue experiments (e.g. feathers, eggshells (well washed), cartons, drinks bottles)

Health and safety

⚠ Careful supervision needed throughout the use of these materials

⚠ Supervision always needed when water is used

ACTIVITY 12

Making pink playdough pigs

Resources you will need

- Mixing bowl, wooden spoons
- 1.5kg plain flour, 500g cooking salt, approximately 750ml water in a jug
- Pink food colouring
- Recipe card for playdough (see p. 88)

Aim/concept

- To make their own playdough, combining ingredients and noting their changes, and using the dough to make pigs

Process

- Explain to the children what they are going to do.
- Let them help weigh the ingredients into the mixing bowl and to each take part in mixing the ingredients to make the dough.
- Give each child a piece of dough to handle. What does it feel like? How is it different to the playdough they often experience (assuming they mostly have the traditional cooked playdough)? i.e. this dough can be broken into chunks, it does not stretch.
- Talk about a pig's shape. Who can describe it?
- Encourage each child to make a pig from their piece of dough.
- Display them on a table. Label the pigs.

Vocabulary/discussion

- Use terms such as mould, handle, roll, break apart, pinch, squeeze, shape
- Talk about size and specific features of the pigs (e.g. ears, snout)

Group size

4–6

Extension idea

Make peppermint cream pigs too.

Health and safety

⚠ Be aware of allergies and provide alternatives if necessary

Links to Foundation Stage Curriculum

PD Explore malleable materials by patting, stroking, poking, squeezing, pinching and twisting them (SS)

ELG Handle tools, objects, construction and malleable materials safely and with increasing control

CD Work creatively on a large or small scale (SS)

ELG Explore colour, texture, shape, form and space in two or three dimensions

The Very Hungry Caterpillar

This delightful tale of a life cycle, from egg to caterpillar to chrysalis to butterfly, is now a firmly established classic. Have fun exploring with your children the concept of change, the days of the week and the opportunities for counting, predicting, creativity and food tasting.

ACTIVITY 13 Make a life cycle storyboard

Resources you will need

- A large board or display area
- Creative materials – coloured paper, tissue paper, material
- Scissors, glue, stapler
- Sequencing sheet (see p. 89)

THE VERY HUNGRY CATERPILLAR
by Eric Carle

Aim/concept

- To explore a life cycle, from egg to caterpillar to pupa to butterfly
  egg → caterpillar → pupa → butterfly

Process

- Divide a display board into four sections. Ask the children to help you with this.

- Talk to them about caterpillars. What can they tell you about them? Do they know how they change? Have they ever seen a chrysalis?
- Show the children pictures in wildlife magazines so that they can see the differences at each stage. Refer back to the story of *The Very Hungry Caterpillar* and how there was initially an egg on a leaf.
- Provide a range of creative resources for the children to make the four stages of the life cycle. Help them negotiate who will create what.
- Be on hand to suggest and support as appropriate.
- Display the life cycle on the board. Encourage the children to work out the correct order in which they need to be displayed.

Vocabulary/discussion

- Use the terms egg, caterpillar, pupa, chrysalis, butterfly, life cycle, cocoon
- Talk about life cycles of other creatures (e.g. tadpoles into frogs)

Group size

4–6

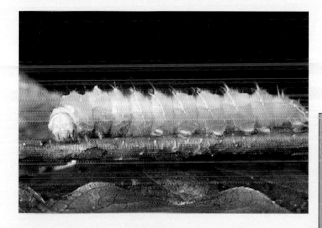

Extension idea

1. Draw caterpillars from observation, either from an appropriately captive specimen or from a picture (see p. 18).
2. Make caterpillar shapes from a range of materials e.g. clay, dough, egg cartons, pipe cleaners.

Links to Foundation Stage Curriculum

PSE Display high levels of involvement in activities (SS)

ELG Continue to be interested, excited and motivated to learn.

CLL Develop emerging self-confidence to speak to others about wants and interests (SS)

ELG Interact with others, negotiating plans and activities and taking turns in conversation

Health and safety

⚠ Careful supervision of scissor use
⚠ Adult only to use stapler

ACTIVITY 14 Butterfly prints

Resources you will need

- Sheets of paper folded in half (the folding is an important part of the activity)
- Dishes of medium thickness paint
- Fingers, brushes or printing objects for designing the butterflies

Aim/concept

- To learn about symmetry and folding techniques

Process

- Show the children pictures of butterflies. What do they notice about them? Guide the children in identifying the symmetry of their wings.
- Explain to the children what they will be doing and give each child a sheet of paper.
- Model for them how to make a central fold in the paper, showing them how to match the edges of the paper and press down on the crease. They are likely to need help with this.

- Provide a range of paint and encourage them to use their fingers, or provide utensils for making the design. Alternatively use brushes or printers.
- Demonstrate how to design using only one half of the paper, folding and pressing down to make the matching image.

Vocabulary/discussion

- Introduce terms such as symmetry, image, mirrored, alike, matching, central
- Discuss actions such as crease, fold, edge, press

Group size

4–6

Extension ideas

1. Provide mirrors for the children to experiment with looking at objects around the setting 'in reverse', i.e. seeing things in symmetry.
2. Make props for telling *The Very Hungry Caterpillar* story.
3. Make caterpillars from two strips of green crepe paper using the over-and-under process in making Christmas decorations.
4. Make a counting display – one apple, two pears and so on.
5. Enjoy a food-tasting activity, pretending to be caterpillars.

Links to Foundation Stage Curriculum

MD	Show awareness of symmetry (SS)
ELG	Talk about, recognise and re-create simple patterns
CD	Explore what happens when they mix colours (SS)
ELG	Explore colour, texture, shape, form and space in two or three dimensions

Health and safety

⚠ Ensure mirrors are made from safety glass

Owl Babies

This delightful story with its beautiful illustrations provides an opportunity to discuss security and emotions. What/who makes each of us feel safe? Why is that? The story also provides great opportunities to link to nocturnal life or woodland animals in general.

ACTIVITY

15 Making owls

Resources you will need

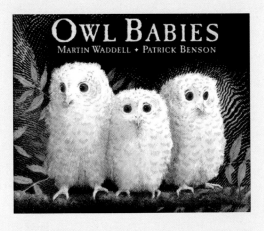

- Cylinder shapes – wide cardboard tubes or similar
- Different shades of brown tissue paper
- Light brown card
- Yellow card
- Scissors
- Glue

Aim/concept

- To make an item using observation skills and, as a group, to use them for counting

Process

- Show the children a picture of an owl (see p. 19), or a soft toy owl. Support them in noting the owl's features (e.g. large eyes, beak, face shape).
- Provide a suitable selection of resources for the children to make their own owls.

- Encourage the children to observe the owl closely as they make their creation, naming features for them if appropriate.
- Display the owls. Help the children to count them and put them into size order.

Vocabulary/discussion

- Name the features of the owl
- Talk about the colour and texture of its feathers
- Discuss where they live (e.g. the woods, on farms, barn owls in barns)

Group size

4–6

Extension ideas

1. Discuss other creatures that are awake at night. Read stories about foxes, badgers and so on.
2. Link to a topic on woodland animals, squirrels, hedgehogs, rabbits, foxes, badgers, pheasants.

Links to Foundation Stage Curriculum

KUW Construct with a purpose in mind, using a variety of resources (SS)

ELG Build and construct using a wide range of objects, selecting appropriate resources, and adapting their work where necessary

CD Make three-dimensional structures (SS)

SS Choose particular colours to use for a purpose

ELG Explore colour, texture, shape, form and space in two or three dimensions

Health and safety

⚠ Careful supervision of scissor use

ACTIVITY 16 Hand printing to make an owl display

Resources you will need

- Thin card or sturdy paper in different shades of brown
- Scissors and glue
- OR dishes of medium thickness paint in browns and cream and a large sheet of paper
- OR crayons in different shades of brown
- Marker pen to draw around hands

Aim/concept

- To increase manipulative dexterity through scissor use and hand printing, colouring and drawing outlines

Process

- Look at a picture of an owl with the children. What colours can they see? Explain that they are going to make an owl, using their hands as feathers.
  Either:
- Demonstrate to the children how to draw around their hands. Let them try this either around their own or around a friend's hand.
- Encourage the children to draw as many hands as possible and then to cut them out. You may need to support them in this.

- Help the children assemble an owl shape using the hand 'feathers'.
- Ask the children to add eyes and a beak to the owl shape. Display prominently once glue has dried.

Or:

- Enjoy making a hand-printed owl with the children, encouraging them to position the feathers in the same direction (downwards).

Vocabulary/discussion

- Introduce terms such as around, image, shape, outline
- Talk about feathers and how they keep the owl warm and dry
- Discuss colours and colour shades

Group size

4–6

Links to Foundation Stage Curriculum

CD Engage in activities requiring hand–eye co-ordination (SS)

SS Use one-handed tools and equipment

ELG Handle tools, objects, construction and malleable materials safely and with increasing control

CD Experiment to create different textures (SS)

ELG Explore colour, texture, shape, form and space in two or three dimensions

Extension ideas

1. Use hand-prints (cut out) to make an individual owl picture, or hand print directly on to an owl shape.
2. Use hand printing to make other designs (e.g. a swan, a rainbow).

Health and safety

⚠ Careful supervision of scissor use

ACTIVITY 17 Making an owl mask

Resources you will need

- Light brown card, wool or elastic
- Scissors, string, hole puncher, hole reinforcers
- Template for owl mask (optional) (p. 90)

Aim/concept

- To make own props for use in a movement session

Process

- Explain to the children that later on they are going to be moving around like owls and other night creatures.
- Ask who would like to make an owl mask – remember that not all children like wearing masks. They could make an owl picture instead.
- Provide sheets of card for them to draw their mask shape on, OR provide ready-cut-out mask shapes using the template on p. 90.
- Support the children in creating their mask and help them to finish it using hole punchers, string and so on.
- In the movement session, encourage the children to swoop and fly, beating their wings (arms) steadily.

Vocabulary/discussion

- Use terms such as swoop, dive, plunge, fly, soar, glide, beat
- Introduce other night creatures (e.g. mice, badgers, foxes), describing their movements: lumber, trudge, plod, skulk, creep, prowl, scurry, scuttle, scamper

Group size

4–6 for making masks
Whole group for movement session

Links to Foundation Stage Curriculum

PD Show respect for other children's personal space when playing among them (SS)

ELG Show awareness of space, of themselves and of others

PD Experiment with different ways of moving (SS)

ELG Move with confidence, imagination and in safety

Extension ideas

1. Make a range of masks and take turns being each nocturnal animal.
2. Use musical instruments to depict daytime and night-time to indicate when to fly and when to 'sleep'.

Health and safety

⚠ Careful supervision of scissor use
⚠ Ensure that enough space is available for children to move around safely

STORY 7

Elmer

This book is simply fun, fun, fun! Children love Elmer and elephants in general. Use it as part of a topic about celebrating difference and also of inclusion and acceptance. Elmer's patchwork coat offers opportunities for colour work and tessellation.

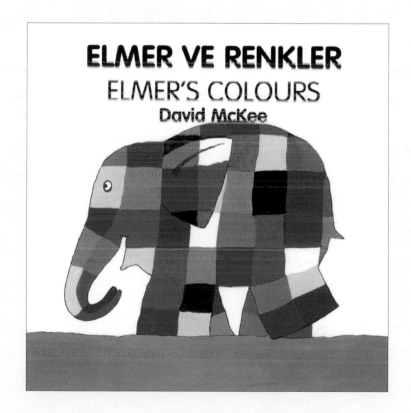

ELMER VE RENKLER
ELMER'S COLOURS
David McKee

ACTIVITY 18 Patchwork pictures

Resources you will need

- Sheets of sturdy paper
  Either:
- Sheets of different colour paper for cutting (you may wish to have some ready prepared for less dexterous children)
- Glue, scissors
  Or:
- A range of paint colours with brushes
- Copies of template of elephant (optional) (p. 91)

Aim/concept

- To explore the use of colour and design while making own Elmer elephant

Process

- Talk about Elmer with the children. What can they tell you about him? What do they like best about him?
- Discuss making Elmer elephants with the children. How might they do this? What do they think they will need?
- Provide a range of resources for them and support them in their creativity.
- Display appropriately.

Vocabulary/discussion

- Talk about the Elmer stories and what happens
- Talk about colours and name any colours which the children do not know
- Talk about patterns and colour matching
- Encourage the children to think about what is different and what is the same about Elmer, compared to other elephants

Group size

4–6

Links to Foundation Stage Curriculum

PD Experiment with different ways of moving (SS)

ELG Move with confidence, imagination and in safety

CD Choose particular colours for a purpose (SS)
Work creatively on a large or small scale (SS)

ELG Explore colour, texture, shape, form and space in two or three dimensions

Extension ideas

1. Paint natural colour elephants too and use as a display.
2. Practise being elephants during a movement session (e.g. trunks swinging, feet plodding)

Health and safety

⚠ Careful supervision of scissor use

ACTIVITY 19 Tessellation

Resources you will need

- A range of accurately cut-out shapes (see templates on p. 92)
- Large sheets of paper

Aim/concept

- To learn how to tessellate, to position shapes accurately to cover a designated area

Process

- Talk about the patchwork 'skin' of Elmer. Are there any gaps between the colours? Explain that this close fit is called tessellation.
- Encourage the children to think where else they have seen tessellation (e.g. patchwork quilts, honeycomb, some footballs, paving).
- Provide resources for the children to practise their tessellation skills. The shapes on p. 92 may be used to make large designs, or you may wish to make smaller shapes for them to 'fill in'.

Group size

6–8 if enough shapes are available

Vocabulary/discussion

- Talk about shapes: square, triangle, hexagon
- Count how many sides each shape has
- Use terms such as next to, alongside, adjacent to, against
- Which shapes can be divided into other shapes?

Links to Foundation Stage Curriculum

- **MD** Show awareness of similarities in shapes in the environment (SS)
- **SS** Use shapes appropriately for tasks
- **ELG** Talk about, recognise and re-create simple patterns
- **KUW** Notice and comment on patterns (SS)
- **ELG** Look closely at similarities, differences, patterns and change

Extension ideas

1. Investigate objects around the setting. What shapes tessellate successfully?
2. Provide a range of different coloured objects (e.g. compare bears (or small coloured elephants if you have them) and create patterns in sequences).

Handa's Surprise

Handa plans a surprise, but gets one herself instead. A delightful story which is great fun, and also lends itself to discussion about other countries and cultures, foods from across the globe and humour.

ACTIVITY 20 Making a fruit salad

Resources you will need

- A range of fruits, some exotic choices if possible
- A little fruit juice, or (slightly sweetened) water in a jug
- Chopping boards, blunt-ended knives, a sharp knife for adult use
- Spoons, a large bowl, smaller bowls or plates
- Recipe for making a fruit salad (p. 93)

Aim/concept

- To explore the taste and texture of a range of fruits, comparing and contrasting their features

Process

- Once hands are washed explore the fruit with the children, handling each fruit in turn.
- Supervise the children as they cut up the fruit for a fruit salad.
- Encourage each child to add their cut-up fruit to the large bowl, stirring it well.
- Let them add juice to the fruit and encourage them to sample each fruit at snack time, discussing which they think were in the *Handa's Surprise* story.

Vocabulary/discussion

- Talk about how each fruit looks, feels, tastes and smells
- Compare ripe and unripe fruit if possible
- What differences can the children see?
- Where does each fruit come from?
- Use terms such as cut, peel, slice, portion, segment, sweet, sour, crunchy, juicy

Group size

4–6

Extension ideas

1. Make fruit juice drinks using a liquidiser or juicer.
2. Use milk to make fruit smoothie drinks.

Links to Foundation Stage Curriculum

KUW Examine objects and living things to find out more about them (SS)

ELG Find out about, and identify, some features of living things, objects and events they observe

PD Understand that tools and equipment have to be used safely (SS)

ELG Handle tools, objects, construction and malleable materials safely and with increasing control

Health and safety

⚠ Supervise hand-washing
⚠ Ensure that all preparation surfaces are cleaned
⚠ Be aware of food allergies and offer alternatives where necessary
⚠ Careful supervision of knife use
⚠ Adult only to use sharp knife
⚠ Ensure that pips, stones and so on are not put into mouths

ACTIVITY 21 Printing with fruit

Resources you will need

- A range of fruits, especially those with interesting insides (e.g. apple, pear, grapefruit, water melon, pomegranate)
- A sharp knife for adult use only
- Large sheets of paper
- Dishes of medium-thickness paint

Aim/concept

- To explore the shape and texture of fruit through the use of paint

Vocabulary/discussion

- Discuss the differences in shape, colour and texture
- Explore terms such as pips, seeds, peel, core

Group size

4–6

Process

- Talk about the fruits you have provided, naming those the children do not know. Cut each fruit in half and explore the inside with the children. What can they see? How do the seeds/pips/stones and so on feel?
- Provide dishes of medium-thickness paint and encourage the children to print with the fruit, noting the patterns made.
- Compare and contrast the designs, linking them back to the fruit halves.

Links to Foundation Stage Curriculum

KUW Sort objects by one function (SS)

ELG Look closely at similarities, differences, patterns and change

CD Work creatively on a large or small scale (SS)

ELG Explore colour, shape, form and space in two or three dimensions

Extension ideas

1. Collect pictures of favourite fruits and share likes and dislikes with the children.
2. Plant pips and seeds from the fruit – observe them to see if they grow.

Health and safety

⚠ Adult only to use sharp knife
⚠ Be aware of food allergies
⚠ Ensure that painted fruits are not eaten

ACTIVITY 22 Tie-dyeing with berries

Resources you will need

- Lengths of muslin or fine cotton material
- Berries such as blackberries
- A large bowl, disposable gloves (optional)
- Small pebbles, rubber bands

Aim/concept

- To explore the concept of using nature to produce colour in design

Process

- Explain to the children that they are going to make a design by dyeing material with the berry juice.
- Using the bowl, crush the berries with the children. Disposable gloves will prevent staining of hands, but will lessen the sensory experience!
- Help the children to wrap up pebbles in various places along the material, securing them tightly with the rubber bands.
- Support the children in immersing the material in the berry juice. Hang out to dry.
- When the material is dry, help the children to remove the pebbles, and admire the design with them.

Vocabulary/discussion

- Use terms such as crush, squash, compress, mash, squeeze
- Discuss the words dye, print, stain, pigment
- Encourage the children to explain what they are seeing and ask them questions

Group size

2–4

Links to Foundation Stage Curriculum

KUW Talk about what is seen and what is happening (SS)

ELG Ask questions about why things happen and how things work

PD Manipulate materials to achieve a planned effect (SS)

ELG Handle tools, objects, construction and malleable materials safely and with increasing control

Health and safety

⚠ Be aware of allergies

Extension ideas

1. Use the dyed cloth for dressing up, or as background for a display on colour, fruit or autumn.
2. Try other natural colour sources (e.g. brown from tea or onion water). Use to dye another length of cloth, or try colouring hard-boiled eggs.

ACTIVITY 23 Drying fruit to use as decorations

Resources you will need

- A range of fruits: apples, oranges, grapefruits and lemons work well and look effective
- A mixture of water and lemon juice to coat the fruit slices
- Chopping boards, round-edged knives for cutting and baking trays
- Sharp knife for adult use only
- Thin ribbon and skewer
- Access to an oven

Aim/concept

- To prepare and dry fruit to make a range of natural decorations for Christmas trees and at other times of celebration

Links to Foundation Stage Curriculum

PSE Have an awareness of, and show interest and enjoyment in, cultural and religious differences (SS)

ELG Understand that people have different needs, views, cultures and beliefs that need to be treated with respect

Group size

4

Process

- Explain to the children that they are going to make some decorations for a Christmas tree or similar festival or celebration.
- Help the children to slice the fruit and cover with the water and lemon juice solution. Lay on baking trays and bake in a low heat oven until completely dry – approximately two to three hours (apples often take the longest).
- When the fruit cools, help the children to make holes in the dried slices with the skewer and hang each fruit decoration on a length of ribbon.

Extension ideas

1. Using (zoo) animal cutters, make salt dough and use as decorations, making a hole for the ribbon before baking.
2. Provide dried fruit, paw paw, guava and so on for the children to try (be allergy aware).

Vocabulary/discussion

- Use terms such as citrus, sour, sharp, acid, bitter
- Talk about festivals and celebrations

Health and safety

⚠ Adult only to use the sharp knife

Visual resources to support story-telling

The following pages provide a range of ideas for making story-time more visual. An overview is given of each type of resource, followed by instructions for making your own wherever practicable:

- Making books with children
- Storyboards
- Story sacks
- Changeable wall displays
- Persona dolls
- Making and using puppets

Making books with children

Making books gives children a special ownership of the end result. Try including this activity following a special trip or a festive occasion to enable children to record observations and memories in a way that is meaningful to them.

Books can be small or large, a group project or an individual activity. Try providing coloured paper sometimes as an alternative to white. Provide card for the covers to improve durability, and consider the use of shaped pages too.

Try folding a sheet of A4 paper to make a small simple multi-page book (refer to the template on p. 94). This also works well with A3 paper.

Books can be bound in a variety of ways. Try staples, punched holes with ribbon or string, comb binding or treasury tags. Draw children's attention to how books are made, discussing issues of durability, and why babies and toddlers need 'tougher' books.

Remember:

Making books uses a range of skills. Fine motor skills are developed as children cut, fold and bind their pages. They will use memory, observation and imagination as they create and design. An interest in writing will be encouraged through labelling and 'writing' of stories or words. A love of books in general will be helped through

the pleasure gained by the children from making books themselves and the interest shown in this process by the adults around them.

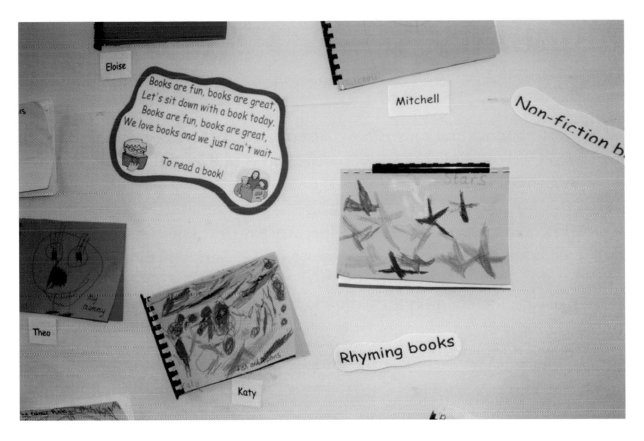

Storyboards

Using a storyboard not only adds a visual element to story time; it can also help increase the concentration span in restless children and those who concentrate better if their hands are occupied.

A storyboard is a surface on which the process of a tale is told gradually by the children, with each taking turns to add the readily available props as the story unfolds. The term may also be used to describe a creative activity asking the children to relate the sequence of the story in their own way on a large sheet of paper or display surface divided into an appropriate number of sections.

Storyboards usually use either magnetic pieces placed on a metalled board, or fabric pieces with Velcro fastenings which attach to a length of felt or a similarly fuzzy fabric. Years ago they were known as flannelgraphs. They are simple to make. Children's involvement in the preparation of the props will mostly be dependent on the simplicity or complexity of the images in the chosen story. They can, however, usually be involved in some way. See suggestions below.

Process

- Select a story with simple pictures, and either draw the main characters and artefacts on to stiff card or cut the appropriate shapes from suitable fabrics. You may need more than one of some pieces.
- Check whether your board surface is magnetic or fuzzy.
- Depending on your board surface, glue either magnetic strips or Velcro 'claws' on to the reverse side of the card or fabric pieces.
- It may be useful to add numbers to the reverse side of each piece to help keep the story flowing.
- As you tell the story, add each prop to support the story-telling.
- Once children understand what storyboards are all about, involve them in plotting the story on the board or cloth as you tell the story. They may want to prompt you as you go along.

- Encourage the children to make storyboards with you, using pictures from magazines or travel brochures (e.g. to tell a story about going shopping or on holiday), or use health pamphlets to talk through a health message.
- The following examples were made by an early years student who used them successfully in a nursery class setting.

Miffy at the Seaside by Dick Bruna

The Three Billy Goats Gruff – traditional

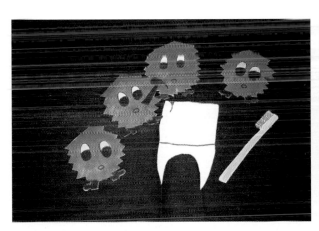

Student's own idea

The Egg by Dick Bruna

Story sacks

Story sacks are a superb resource for any early years and primary setting. They are great fun to use, and provide a visually appealing and educational means of encouraging children and their families to read, and to enjoy stories together.

The concept of a story sack was first promoted commercially by Neil Griffiths, with Storysack Ltd now producing an enormous range of props to support the sharing of many favourite and traditional tales.

Story sacks contain a range of artefacts relevant to the featured story which may be enjoyed either as a group time within the setting, or by being loaned out to parents to further enhance the sharing of books at home as a family. Each story sack includes a parent guidance sheet.

The exploration of story sack resources helps children's understanding of the story and its wider background through music, games, puppets, factual books, and much, much more.

Training and guidance is available for those who wish to make their own story sacks. There is a DVD featuring Neil Griffiths leading workshops in using story sacks (see contact details on p. 96).

The photographs featured here include examples of Storysack Ltd's commercially produced sacks, together with samples of their other products. There are examples of some home-made story sacks too.

Examples of products available from Storysack Ltd

See p. 96 for Storysack Ltd details.

The following story sacks have been made by Annette Walkey, full-time nursery nurse at Little Bridges Nursery, Wadebridge Community Primary School, Wadebridge, Cornwall. Her wonderful creations are used regularly in the nursery and through to key stage 1.

Annette first became interested in making story sacks after attending a course run by Neil Griffiths. She bought a few basic props from Storysack Ltd, enlisted help and artefacts from parents and other staff, and produced these wonderful resources. Aren't they brilliant?

Changeable wall displays

Wall displays are a celebration of the process of children's work and creativity. They brighten up early years settings, and give parents and carers an opportunity to see what their children have been doing as well as demonstrating to the children that what they do is valued. They may be linked to both stories and rhymes, as well as to general topic work, festive occasions or the time of year.

Wall displays can also provide great opportunities for developing children's observation skills. Try making changes to a display in between sessions. The changes you make may be obvious, as with the following example, or more subtle. Perhaps little Bo Peep's sheep reappeared overnight, an extra speckled frog had jumped into the pool, or Incy Wincy spider climbed higher up his spout. The possibilities are endless, but what they each have in common is that they encourage children to look and to think, and to observe change.

As the following example shows, the children in this nursery made a wonderful Humpty Dumpty, and a wall for him to sit on. They enjoyed looking at the wall display and singing the appropriate nursery rhyme.

BUT...

One morning when they arrived, Humpty Dumpty had fallen from his wall and had broken in two. This caused great excitement among the children, who rushed to tell others what had happened. Practitioners followed up this excitement by setting the children a challenge: How could they put Humpty Dumpty back together again? As the last photograph in the sequence shows, they decided on sticky tape.

I first 'allowed' Humpty Dumpty to fall from a display more than 30 years ago. It worked brilliantly then, and has done so every time since.

Persona dolls

Promoting self-esteem is an important part of an early years practitioner's role, ensuring that children feel valued. Persona dolls are an ideal way to help support this. Children learn prejudice from what they see and hear around them, and at three and four years old they may well have heard many examples of prejudice and stereotyping. These dolls may be used successfully to introduce difference in a positive way, and to integrate children smoothly into new situations. They also help the established children in the setting to understand and accept any difference positively.

As an adult introduces a persona doll to a group of children, setting out the doll's background, they will, through discussion and questioning, encourage the children's ability to identify and discuss issues of acceptance, to explore similarities and difference, and help them begin to challenge any biased messages they may have already picked up from prior experience.

> Persona dolls are special dolls with their own personalities, life histories, likes and dislikes. Children readily accept them as small friends. They provide a powerful tool for exploring, uncovering and confronting racism and other social inequalities. They enable children to appreciate that words and actions can be hurtful, to empathise with people experiencing discrimination and to want to stand up and show their support.
>
> www.persona-doll-training.org

Persona dolls may be purchased commercially, or you can make them yourself. In fact any doll may be introduced as a persona doll. It is important, however, to ensure that any dolls you make yourself or select from a general range are sensitively thought through, are made from high-quality materials and that any specific features are accurately portrayed.

It will be absolutely vital to make a note of your dolls' backgrounds, particularly if you have more than one, including their personal details, those of their family and information specific to them (e.g. their culture, special festivals, specific items of clothing worn daily and occasionally). Any specified disabilities or social situation should be noted too, and explained and discussed, noting the positives of what the doll can do, rather than focusing on what may prove to be challenging for them. In the same way, situations involving anxiety, jealousy or anger can be equally well experienced by the doll, helping children to put their own emotions into context, and reassuring them that others feel the same way as they do. Through your discussion with and about the persona doll the children will be helped to manage their emotions and express them more positively.

The following website gives details and contacts for Babette Brown's persona doll training: www.persona-doll-training.org

Making and using puppets

Puppets can be wonderful props in any setting, both as a source of great fun and as a versatile support to learning at any stage within early years and across all areas of the Foundation Stage Curriculum. Babies will focus keenly on a clear face or bold eyes, and laugh readily at a waving hand or paw. Children who are reluctant to converse with adult practitioners, or even their peers, will often feel able to talk to and through a puppet, sharing their thoughts and feelings with them. This can help boost the confidence of the shy child and provide a communication channel for the child with worries or concerns. Practitioners can set the puppets a task to achieve, and ask the children to provide guidance for them, involving them in projects and special events across each area of learning. Puppets are also brilliant as a prop for imaginative play.

Commercially there are many wonderful puppets to choose from, and companies such as the Puppet Company offer a mail order service (see p. 96 for details), making them very accessible. It is important to remember too that home-made puppets can have a great deal of value as well, with the additional benefit of the children's involvement in their creation. These will of course be less durable, and most likely will have a short life span, but encouraging children to work in collaboration with each other, in making them or in talking to or entertaining each other, helps develop a range of social skills so important to their development.

Puppets can be of almost any size. Finger puppets enable intimate story-telling and multiple child involvement. They are simple to make, too. Huge puppets are often a favourite in busy classrooms where the relevant puppet visits regularly and brings the whole group together in a very positive way. At times puppets have even helped busy practitioners maintain a controlled environment. I have known a reception class teacher who claimed her toucan (puppet) had better control of the class than she did some days.

Using puppets involves a variety of fine motor skills, as hands and fingers help puppets to wave, speak and gesture. The use of string puppets helps children to learn about cause and effect, but can take a while for small hands to gain the appropriate level of control needed for successful use.

If you have never used a puppet before, give it a try. Children will love it, and the experience will no doubt be great fun for you, too.

Remember:

Puppets can be made from the simplest of resources (e.g. paper bags, cardboard tubes and old socks). All you need is time and a little imagination.

Have a go at some of the suggestions on pp. 73–82.

'Living' puppets

The wonderful 'living' puppets featured below offer opportunities for the puppet to really become part of the group. Their large size and fun characteristics will fill children with both awe and wonder. Few children remain uninterested in puppets with this type of physical presence. The potential for them to be expressive, communicative and joyous in the hands of the puppeteer is enhanced by the easy animation of head, mouth and hands.

The greatest fun and benefit to children is when these puppets become regular visitors to the setting. Children begin to anticipate their arrival when they see the familiar container in which the puppet lives, and practitioners soon find that the puppet helps them to discuss problems, introduce new concepts and share news.

Useful tips for presenting 'living' puppets

- Practise first until you feel confident. Try watching yourself in a mirror, but remember that, when starting out, you will almost certainly feel more awkward than you look.
- Present the puppet to the children from its special home, rather than just getting it out of your usual bag from among your other possessions. The puppet's home could be a trendy bag or a small suitcase, a box, or a drawstring bag made from an exciting material. Anything really, so long as it is special to the puppet and easily recognised by the children.
- Ensure your puppet is 'alive' when it is introduced to the children. Practise getting it on and off your arm discreetly.
- Ensure the puppets are still seen to be 'alive' when they are being put back into their special home.
- Give the puppets their own background and personality. Children will love knowing all about them, their likes and dislikes, mood and temperament. (NB: A living puppet may be introduced in much the same way as a persona doll.) In the book *Puppets at Large* (see p. 95 for details), Linda Bentley describes this process as creating the puppet profile. She wisely warns practitioners to learn the facts about their puppet well, as children have very good memories for such detail.

Budding puppeteers can learn a great deal of practical handling advice from *Puppets at Large*, for example:

- A puppet's small shaking head movements up and down can depict suppressed or mischievous laughter.
- Chin down can depict sadness, sulking or shyness.
- Head low and facing away from you can depict feeling rejected.
- A slow wave close to the body can depict a shy greeting.
- A hand on heart can depict great depth of feeling or a pleasant surprise.

As a practitioner it is important to settle the children around you before you introduce the puppet. Ensure that all the children will be able to see you both. Support the puppet in looking at each child in turn. This will help all the children to feel involved and encourage the shyest children to participate.

Remember:

A puppet can have an enormous influence on young children. Choose your words and actions carefully and always use your puppet in a positive way.

See resources list on p. 96 for further details.

Paper bag puppets

These are probably the most basic of all puppets. You simply need to provide a paper bag for each child and the resources for the children to make a face, be it a person, an animal or a monster of their choosing.

The benefits of paper bag puppets are that they are cheap and so easy to use. Children will make them spontaneously if the relevant resources are supplied.

Springy puppets

These springy puppets are made through a simple folding and cutting process. It can be tempting to use card to increase durability, but this can restrict the puppet's 'springy-ness'.

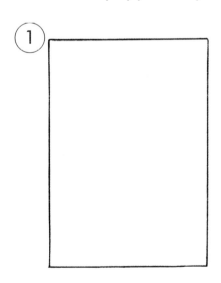

①

② Fold in half and draw half of puppet outline

③ Cut out shape and cut three-quarters of the way across

④ Add facial features and so on

⑤ Punch a hole at top of puppet and thread with string to hang

Children will enjoy jumping and dancing these puppets together.

  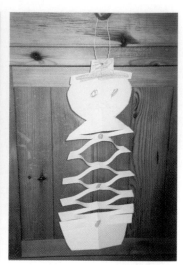

Sock puppets

Take a plain washed sock, or cut down a pair of tights and simply add your own features to your puppet's head. Either embroider features in thread of a contrasting colour, or glue fabric pieces in the appropriate places.

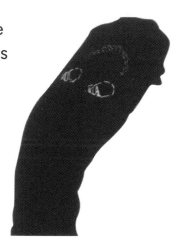

The puppet featured opposite is 'Worm'. His simple embroidered facial features held the attention of his owner, baby Jasmine, for long periods of time. He chased, captured and tickled her, which she loved. As a young toddler she would contentedly put Worm on her own arm and be very pleased with herself. As an active two-year-old (with Worm on her arm) she enjoyed chasing, capturing and tickling other people.

This was joyful puppet play in its simplest form.

Paper plate puppets

These are simple puppets that children can enjoy creating for themselves and which they can easily use within imaginary play. Try using them to illustrate a rhyme or simple story as well (e.g. duck faces could be used to support the singing 'Five little ducks went swimming one day', monkey faces could support singing 'Five little monkeys jumping on the bed').

Each puppet needs one whole paper plate and one half.

The puppet's features are set out on the main plate using resources of your choice, and the half plate is fastened to the back, leaving a raised gap for the child's hand, as in this photograph.

String puppets

String puppets are not always easy for young children to handle, but they will still enjoy trying, and they will have fun constructing their puppets with the help of a practitioner. These puppets help the children to learn about cause and effect, as the strings are raised and the corresponding arms and legs move. String puppets encourage the development of fine motor skills, but require quite an advanced level of control to be fully successful.

For each puppet, you will need cotton reels or short lengths of cardboard tubes. A short piece of dowling rod makes a good bar for the strings to be attached to. For very young children it is easier to just have the one dowling rod. Older children may be able to cope with the crossed-over style of a traditional marionette.

■ Agree with the children how many cotton reels or cardboard tube lengths they will need for each part of the puppet's body.

■ The legs will need to be threaded up through the main body and secured at the neck – remember to leave a little slack for the knee joints. Strings will be added here and joined to the dowling rod.

■ The arms can be threaded through the middle of the body pieces, securing them together in the middle. Again, the strings need to be attached to the dowling rod.

■ A shorter string will be attached to the head, and also to the dowling rod.

■ When all parts have been secured, children can enjoy walking and dancing their puppets together.

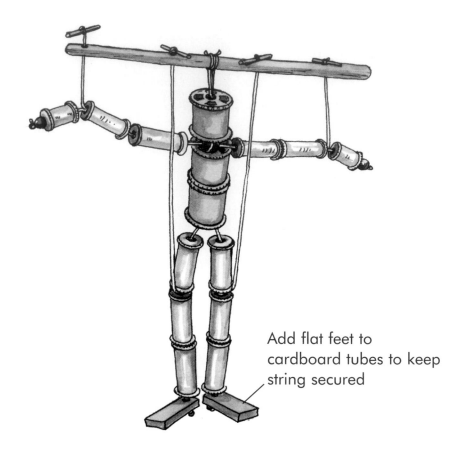

Add flat feet to
cardboard tubes to keep
string secured

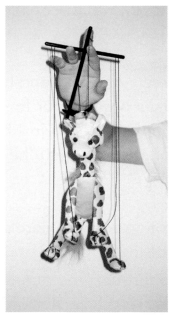

Hand puppets

Hand puppets are simply great fun. They are such reasonable prices
nowadays that having a selection is affordable in many settings. Children
love the cosiness of handling the puppets. They are often very cuddly and
almost always appealing.

When you have introduced a puppet to the children you can ask them questions and share news and ideas with them, possibly without the puppet ever saying a word – except in your ear of course. Children will often listen very intently to try and hear them!

Hand puppets can be either child hand size or adult hand size. It is good to have samples of each. Puppets which are initially hidden (see rabbit in lettuce below) are great fun, and the mini-beasts found within the lettuce leaves cause great excitement and are also (finger) puppets themselves (see resources list on p. 96 for stockist details).

Hand puppets can be fun to make with young children, and are a great opportunity to introduce simple sewing skills, too.

- You will need some soft, easily sewn-on fabric – felt is ideal – together with large bodkin needles and balls of wool.
- Draw around the child's hand twice and cut out a basic puppet shape (as illustrated below) a little larger than the hand shape. Help the children to cut out these shapes.

- Let the children add features of their choice to their puppet (e.g. face, buttons, clothes).
- Encourage and support the children in sewing around the shaped edge of the puppet, securing the stitches firmly at each side.

Children will enjoy talking to and through their puppets.

Spoon puppets

What can be simpler than drawing a face on a wooden spoon? Indelible ink can be useful here as it will not smudge or come off.

- Try making a happy/sad spoon.
- Provide different sized spoons and encourage the children to make props for stories such as *Goldilocks and the Three Bears*.
- Use spoons as a basis for quick and easy pop-up puppets.

Shadow puppets

This type of puppetry can really capture children's interest, as they look at the shapes they make with their hands, and manipulate the puppets they make. They will learn about the use of light too, and will enjoy playing shadows outside on sunny days.

- You will need to set up a screen for the shadows to be seen against. A white sheet is ideal.
- If you have access to an overhead projector, place it behind the sheet. Torches may be used instead if necessary.
- Help the children to make simple puppet shapes and attach them to sticks, or lengths of dowling rod.
- Demonstrate how to make shadows. Encourage the children to experiment with their hands, too.

Finger puppets

These tiny puppets both amuse and intrigue young children. Try providing a whole selection to help inspire children to initiate their own stories and performances. Finger puppets can be used to retell a favourite story (e.g. *Red Riding Hood*, *The Three Little Pigs*). Commercial puppet companies sell a wonderful range to support the retelling of many traditional and favourite stories, but you can make them too.

- Make cone shapes from a sheet of card and dress the shapes up as simple puppets (e.g. mice, cats).
- Cut the fingers off old pairs of gloves and sew on facial features and clothing.
- Use felt shapes a little bigger than your finger and sew around the edges, adding a range of features.

It may be helpful to keep sets of puppets together in a cloth bag, or on a cardboard hand shape – one on each finger. Cut this out from stiff card. Your hand can always have an extra finger or two! No one will mind.

Pop-up puppets

Pop-up puppets are all about surprise, and they cause much fun and laughter. They are easy to make, too. You simply need a yoghurt-type pot or a disposable beaker, material, a stick and a cotton reel, plus resources for the puppet's details (e.g. clothing, face and body features).

- Cut two hand puppet shapes from a piece of material (as for the hand puppet on pp. 78–79). Make sure they will be wide enough to fit around the widest rim of the yoghurt pot once joined together at the sides, and long enough to be able to be pulled down to the bottom of the pot without pressure.
- Sew the sides of the puppet securely.
- Secure a knob on to the end of the stick with strong glue. This could be a cotton reel or a large wooden bead.
- Push the stick up into the puppet's head and stuff wadding or extra material around it. Secure the head by tying it tightly at the neck.
- Secure the bottom edge of the puppet to the rim of your pot with glue and strong tape. This can be reinforced by tying strong thread around the rim. The puppet is now ready to hide and reappear.

Photocopiable sheets

Use the following pages and templates to support the activities and resources set out in this book.

Links to Activity 1 (p. 24)
The Giant Jam Sandwich

Links to Activity 3 (p. 26)
The Gingerbread Man

A child's recipe card for making gingerbread men.

Gingerbread people – makes about 12

Ingredients:

- 350g (12oz) plain flour
- 5ml (1 level teaspoon) bicarbonate of soda
- 10 ml (2 level teaspoons) ground ginger
- 125g (4oz) margarine
- 175g (6oz) brown sugar
- 1 egg, broken up lightly with a fork
- 4 tablespoons golden syrup
- Currants or raisins or sweets for facial features and buttons

Utensils:

- Scales for weighing ingredients
- Sieve and spoons
- Large mixing bowl
- Floured board for rolling out the biscuit dough
- Rolling-pin
- People-shaped cutters
- Baking trays

Method:

1. Sieve the flour, bicarbonate of soda and ginger into the mixing bowl.
2. Add the margarine and mix until crumbly.
3. Stir in the sugar.
4. Add the egg.
5. Add the golden syrup and mix to a firm dough.
6. Roll out on to the floured board and cut into people shapes with the cutters.
7. Bake on baking trays for approximately 15 minutes at 190°C/375°F or Gas Mark 5
8. Make faces and add buttons, using the dried fruit.

Links to Activity 6 (p. 31)
Goldilocks and the Three Bears

A child's recipe card for making porridge.

Porridge

Ingredients:

- 1 large mug of porridge oats
- 2 to 3 large mugs of milk
- 2 tablespoons brown sugar or honey

Utensils:

- Access to a microwave
- A microwaveable bowl
- A wooden spoon
- A small bowl for each child
- A spoon for each child

Method:

1. Measure the ingredients into the bowl.
2. Let everyone have a stir.
3. Microwave on high for 1 minute.
4. Remove from microwave and stir well.
5. Microwave on high again for 1 minute.
6. Stir again, and repeat process as needed at 20-second intervals until cooked to required consistency.

Remember:

The porridge will be very hot. Allow to cool to a safe temperature before it is served to the children.

Links to Activity 8 (p. 33)
Goldilocks and the Three Bears

Links to Activity 12 (p. 39)
The Three Little Pigs

Playdough recipe – non-stretchy dough

Ingredients:

- 1.5kg (3lb) plain flour
- 500g (1lb) cooking salt
- Approximately 750ml (1 pint) water
- Pink food colouring

Utensils:

- A large mixing bowl
- Weighing scales
- A measuring jug for the water
- A wooden spoon

Method:

1. Weigh the ingredients.
2. Combine the flour and salt in a large bowl.
3. Gradually add the water.
4. Add in a small drop of food colouring. Mix.
5. Knead well to obtain a smooth texture.

This dough will break cleanly. It holds its shape well, and can be pulled apart into small pieces and squashed back together again. It does not stretch.

Links to Activity 13 (p. 40)
The Very Hungry Caterpillar

Links to Activity 17 (p. 48)
Owl Babies

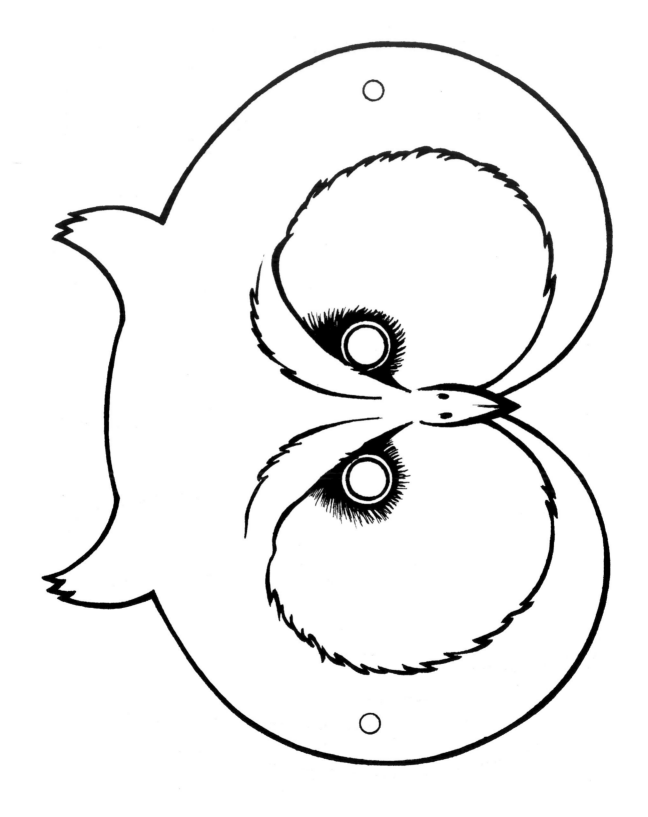

Links to Activity 18 (p. 50)
Elmer

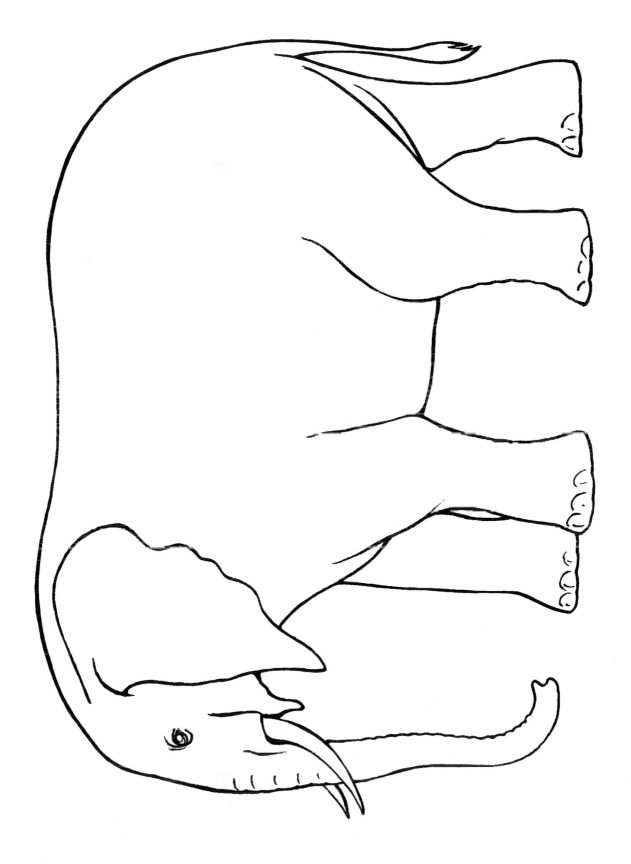

Links to Activity 19 (p. 52)
Elmer

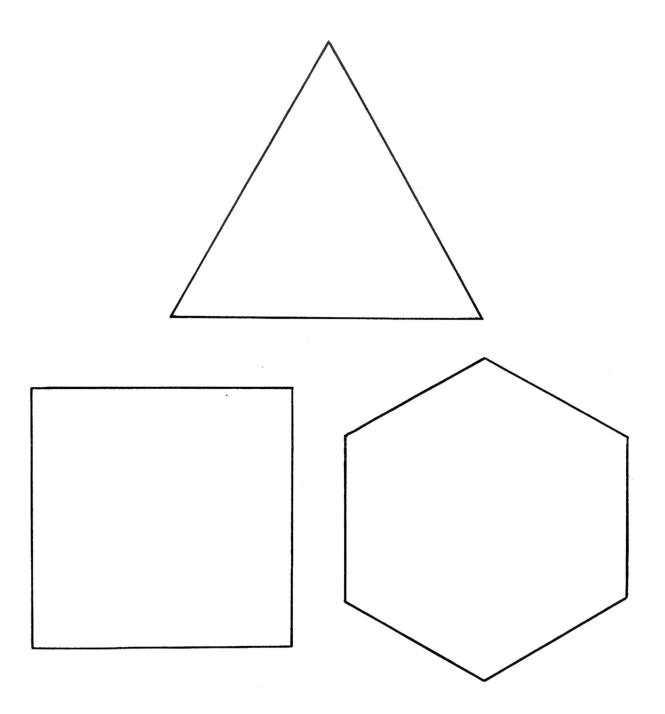

Links to Activity 20 (p. 54)
Handa's Surprise

A child's recipe card for making a fruit salad.

Fruit salad

Ingredients:

- A range of fruits
- Fruit juice, or water slightly sweetened

Utensils:

- Boards for cutting the fruit
- Knives
- A large bowl, and small bowls for each child
- A ladle for serving
- Spoons for eating the fruit

Method:

1. Each child to select a fruit to cut up, or several pieces of fruit to cut up further.
2. Add cut-up fruits to the large bowl.
3. Add a little juice to the large bowl. Mix well.
4. Ladle fruit into small bowls for each child.
5. Enjoy!

Links to Making Books with Children (p. 60)

1. An A4 sheet held landscape.

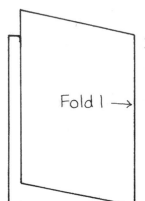

2. Fold the A4 sheet in half, with the fold on the right.

Fold 1 →

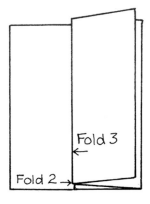

Fold 3 ←

Fold 2 →

3. Fold the two sides outwards towards the central fold. Open the furthest side out again. You should now have one layer of paper on the left and three on the right.

4. Fold in half towards you.

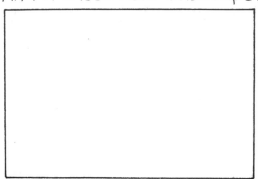

Fold 4

5. Open up again (as in stage 2 with fold again on your right). Cut halfway along the horizontal fold, from the right to the left.

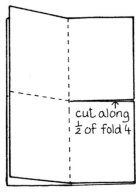

cut along ½ of fold 4

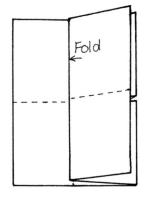

Fold ←

6. Fold as in stage 3. You should have one layer of paper on the left and three layers on the right.

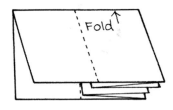

Fold ↑

7. Fold in half downwards, towards you once again.

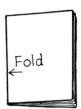

Fold ←

8. Fold in half again sideways to form a book shape.

Resources

Further reading

Linda Bentley (2005), *Puppets at Large* (Wiltshire: Positive Press)

Babette Brown (2001), *Combating Discrimination: Persona Dolls in Action* (Trentham Books)

Eileen Browne (1994), *Handa's Surprise* (London: Walker Books)

Dick Bruna (n.d.), *The Egg* (London: Methuen Children's Books)

Dick Bruna (2003) *Miffy at the Seaside* (London: Egmont)

Eric Carl (2002), *The Very Hungry Caterpillar* (Harmondsworth: Picture Puffin)

David McKee (1990), *Elmer's Colours* (London: Milet) shown in English–Turkish

Marcus Pfister, (2001) *The Rainbow Fish* (North–South Books) shown in English–French

Michael Rosen and Helen Oxenbury (2001), *We're Going on a Bear Hunt* (London: Walker Books)

Gwenyth Swain (2000), *Carrying* (Milet) shown in English–Urdu

Georgia Thorp (2005), *The Power of Puppets* (Wiltshire: Positive Press)

Traditional tale *The Three Little Pigs*

Traditional tale *The Three Bears*

Traditional tale *The Gingerbread Man*

David Tsai, *George's Garden* (2000), (London: Milet) shown in English–Chinese

Sedat Turhan and Sally Hagin (2003), *Mini Picture Dictionary* (London: Milet) shown in English–French

Sedat Turhan and Sally Hagin (2003), *Picture Dictionary* (London: Milet) shown in English–Bengali; English–Korean

Elfrida Vipont and Raymond Briggs (1971), *The Elephant and the Bad Baby* (Harmondsworth: Picture Puffin)

Martin Waddell and Patrick Beason (1992), *Owl Babies* (London: Walker Books)

Useful sources of multicultural and dual language books

Letterbox Library
www.letterboxlibrary.com

Mantra Lingua Publishers
www.mantralingua.com

Milet Publishing
www.milet.com

Tamarind
www.tamarindbooks.co.uk

Other resources

In addition, try the following companies for a range of useful resources to support story-telling and imaginative play:

The Puppet Company
www.puppetsbypost.com

Storysack Ltd
www.storysack.com